THE LONDON TAXI

Nick Georgano and Bill Munro

SHIRE PUBLICATIONS

This edition first published in Great Britain in 2008 by Shire Publications Ltd, Midland House, West Way, Botley, Oxford OX2 0PH, United Kingdom.
443 Park Avenue South, New York, NY 10016, USA.

E-mail: shire@shirebooks.co.uk www.shirebooks.co.uk

A CIP catalogue record for this book is available from the British Library.

Shire Library no. 150 • ISBN-13: 978 0 7478 0692 9

Nick Georgano and Bill Munro have asserted their right under the Copyright, Designs and Patents Act, 1988, to be identified as the authors of this book.

Designed by Ken Vail Graphic Design, Cambridge, UK and typeset in Perpetua and Gill Sans.
Printed in Malta by Gutenberg Press Ltd.

08 09 10 11 12 10 9 8 7 6 5 4 3 2 1

COVER IMAGE
Four taxis from the London General Cab Company museum: from left, Austin FX4, Austin FX3, Austin Heavy 12/4, Unic 12/16.

TITLE PAGE IMAGE
The leading illustration from the Morris-Commercial 'Super Six' brochure.

CONTENTS PAGE IMAGE
Illustration from the Nuffield Oxford brochure.

ACKNOWLEDGEMENTS
The authors wish to thank the following for permission to reproduce the photographs in this book:

Nick Georgano pages 5, 35, and 43 (bottom) (National Motor Museum Library); Bryan Goodman, 13 (top), 14 (left), and 21 (bottom); Andrew Hall pages 20 (top), and 25; Ben Hogan collection page 62; LTI Vehicles Ltd pages 54, 58, 59, 60 (top & bottom) (The Fairway and TX shape are registered designs. Fairway ™, TX™ the LTI device, LTI logo and London Taxis International are all trademarks of LTI Ltd); KPM-UK Plc page 61; London Transport Museum pages 28 and 29 (bottom); London Vintage Taxi Association pages 24 (bottom), 41 (bottom), and 44; Ian McLean page 13 (bottom); Bill Munro pages 14 (right), 20 (bottom), 21 (side), 24 (top), 27 (bottom right), 34 (top and side), 35 (top), 37 (side), 42 (top), 43 (top), 45 (top), 46, 48 (top), and 49 (bottom); The National Motor Museum pages 7, 11 (bottom), 16, 19 (top right), 29 (top), 35 (lower), 40 (centre), and 43 (middle); Derek Pearce page 41 (top); Roy Perkins page 32 (top); Public Carriage Office page 11 (centre); Stanley Roth page 10 (top); Barney Sharratt pages 40 (top), 49 (centre), and 51 (lower); Taximedia Ltd page 53; Taxi Newspaper Archive pages 51 (top), 52 (top right), and 57 (both); Stephen Tillyer page 52 (top left & right); Vintage Taxi Spares, cover image and pages 6, 8, 10 (lower), 19 (top), 19 (bottom), 21 (top), 27 (top), 36 (bottom), 38, 40 (bottom), 45 (bottom), 48 (centre), 49 (top); Worshipful Company of Hackney Carriage Drivers pages 4, 11 (top), 32 (bottom), 34 (bottom).

Those on the title page, contents page and pages 17, 22, 26 (bottom), 27 (bottom left), 30, 33 and 42 (bottom) are from Nick Georgano's collection.

Those on pages 12, 15, 18, 26 (top), 27 (bottom, left), 32 (side), 36 (top), and 37 (top) are from Bill Munro's collection.

CONTENTS

INTRODUCTION

The Public Carriage Office at Scotland Yard. Horse cabs were licensed here from 1875 until 1891, when the Metropolitan Police were moved to a new home at New Scotland Yard. Motor cabs were licensed there until 1927, when the PCO was moved to a new Metropolitan Police building in Lambeth Road, south London.

TAXI! Call the word as you raise your arm at the kerbside in London's Park Lane or Piccadilly and you convey a sense of importance, and you might feel it too, for inside a London taxi you have your own private limousine, if for just a few minutes. So once settled, sit back and enjoy being transported (and occasionally lectured!) by one of the most professional taxi drivers in the world, through one of the world's most historic cities.

And, if confronted by a traffic hold-up, your driver spins the cab around seemingly in its own length, you will have benefited from one of the features that makes London cabs special. For as well as having these exceptional men, and these days women too, behind the wheel, London is unique in having purpose-built taxicabs that comply with the strictest licensing regime in the world.

The cabs have evolved from the very first coaches offered for hire in about 1620 by a certain Captain Baily by the May Pole in Charing Cross, at the western end of the Strand. A good idea, especially a profitable one, is always copied and within a few years there were over one hundred of these coaches, clogging the city's narrow streets. They were known as hackney coaches, from the French *hacquenée*, meaning a horse hired out for journeys. The coaches were often cast-offs from the nobility and as their numbers grew their quality fell, earning them the soubriquet of 'hackney hell carts'. Oliver Cromwell introduced a form of licence for them and the men who drove them, under the auspices of a new organisation, the Fellowship of Master Hackney Coachmen. It was the beginning of a long and almost unbroken line of licensing. Notable was the introduction in 1679 of a

set of rules called the Conditions of Fitness, written to ensure the coaches were of a suitable size, were not rotting away and did not have seats stuffed with hay, paper or even seaweed or whalebone shavings, so that well-to-do Londoners could enjoy the same standards in a hackney coach that they took for granted in other walks of life.

In 1694 the Hackney Coach Office was founded, but, after more than a century in which the responsibility for hackney coaches was shuffled between government departments, it was decided in 1834 to hand the task to a more localised body. The Metropolitan Board of Works, the only body overseeing London's many parishes and boroughs, was known to be corrupt, so the task was passed to the Metropolitan Police, the only unimpeachable statutory body with jurisdiction over the entire region of London. The police held that duty, through the Public Carriage Office (PCO), until 2001, when the newly formed Greater London Authority took control of the Metropolitan Police and moved the PCO to the guardianship of Transport for London.

Where did the names 'taxi' and 'cab' come from? The word 'cab' is an abbreviation of the French word *cabriolet*, meaning a light, two-wheeled carriage with a folding hood. The same word is used for modern soft-top cars. First seen in London in 1823, cabriolets were popular for their speed and the name caught on for all types of hackney carriage.

'Taxi' comes from 'taximeter', or 'taxameter', as the mechanical device for accurately measuring a cab fare was originally known. The portmanteau word 'taxicab' was an American invention, coined by Harry N. Allen, who, having been overcharged in 1907 by a Manhattan cab driver, started his own cab company in New York City. He bought a fleet of red Darracqs from France and fitted them with meters so that the customers knew exactly what they had to pay. As a way of catching the public's attention, he called them 'taxicabs'.

A cabmen's shelter in Brompton Road. The first shelter was put up in 1874, in order to give cabmen a place for food, drink and rest other than in public houses. Many fell into disrepair or were destroyed during the Second World War, whilst others disappeared in road-widening schemes. The thirteen that survive are all listed buildings.

MR BERSEY'S ELECTRIC CABS

THROUGHOUT the reign of Queen Victoria, the citizens of London could hail two types of cab. One was the two-wheeled hansom, called 'the gondola of London' by Prime Minister Benjamin Disraeli. It was fast and considered racy by the more staid matrons, who preferred the four-wheeled 'growler', a much slower cab that worked the railway stations because of its luggage-carrying capacity.

Petrol-powered Benz cabs had appeared in Stuttgart and Paris in 1896, but the first horseless cabs to be used in London were electric. They were introduced in August 1897 by the London Electrical Cab Company Ltd of Juxon Street, Lambeth. The company was backed by several prominent men in the transport world, including H.R. Paterson, a director of the goods carriers Carter, Paterson & Company Ltd, and the Honourable Evelyn Ellis,

A hansom cab. The vehicle we know by that name was actually a complete redesign of Joseph Hansom's original model in 1836 by John Chapman. The hansom has become as much an icon of Victorian London as the Austin FX4 has of the late-twentieth-century capital.

a pioneer motorist who the year before had succeeded in getting Parliament to repeal the 1865 Locomotives Act, the so-called 'Red Flag Act', which required that a man with a red flag should walk in front of a horseless carriage. In doing so, Ellis and his colleagues paved the way for motor cars to be used not only for pleasure but for business as well. The cabs were designed by an electrical engineer, Walter C. Bersey, who gave his name to them, but they were known to all as 'humming birds' because of the noise made by the motor. They had a maximum speed of 9 mph, which was fast for a light gig, let alone a cab. Their range was 30 miles, which was much more than a cab horse would have travelled in a day's work.

By the end of 1897 there were twenty-five Bersey cabs running in London, and a further fifty were added in 1898. At first they were well received by the press and public, but, after six months of use, vibrations and rattles set in and the battery boxes became loose. In April 1898 an improved model appeared, but when one ran out of control their popularity evaporated and hirings dropped off. Running costs proved much greater than anticipated and in August 1899 the company was liquidated. A few of the cabs were operated by private owners, but by June 1900 the last of these had been taken off the streets.

The Bersey electric cab. The first examples had bodies by the Great Horseless Carriage Company, while later bodies were built by the Gloucester Railway Carriage & Wagon Company. Of the seventy-five Bersey cabs made, only one is known to survive, in the National Motor Museum at Beaulieu, Hampshire.

THE EDWARDIAN ERA

UNTIL December 1903 the horse cabs had the streets to themselves once more. Then the London Express Motor Service Ltd introduced a two-cylinder 12 hp French-built Prunel motor hansom. It and two more were put on test and in May 1904 they were the first motor cabs to be licensed by the Metropolitan Police Public Carriage Office at Scotland Yard. Early in 1905 they were joined by the first British make, the Rational, and later by another British cab, the London-made Simplex. The London Express was reformed as the Metropolitan Motor Cab & Carriage Company, but, rather than buy more Prunels, they introduced the disastrous Vauxhall hansom, whose driver was perched high up behind the passengers. Fortunately, only three seemed to have been delivered as, according to contemporary reports, they were unnerving to the passengers. Metropolitan subsequently replaced them with a number of French Hérald cabs but, as is often the way with pioneers, Metropolitan foundered.

The Richard-Brasier, introduced to London by motor dealers Mann & Overton's of Pimlico, contributed to an increase in the number of motor cabs from nineteen at the end of 1905 to ninety-six a year later, but despite efforts to attract investors into the business there were few takers. Then the General Motor Cab Company Ltd built a massive garage in Brixton, south London, and ordered five hundred Renault Type AG cabs from Paris. Now, with a big player in the game, others took notice.

In March 1906 a new set of Conditions of Fitness for motor cabs was issued by the Public Carriage Office, written by W. Worby Beaumont, who was recommended by Lord Montagu. The regulations caused an outcry from the Society of Motor Manufacturers and Traders, who thought some of the rules were too difficult to meet, particularly the maximum turning circle of 25 feet, a rule specified to allow a cab to turn without performing a three-point turn and possibly stalling, which would require the cabman to crank the starting handle and cause a traffic jam. Others seem odd today, such as a minimum ground clearance of 10 inches, which would, if some poor soul were to be hit by a cab, allow it to run over him safely without harming him.

Opposite:
We cannot know what these two cabmen are discussing, but as human nature does not change, a likely guess is that older man is telling the younger how the trade has gone downhill since the arrival of motors!

Right: A Prunel hansom ranks up behind two hansoms at Hyde Park Corner. The large house next to the park gates is 'Number 1, London', Apsley House, the former home of the Duke of Wellington.

Below right: Two Rational cabs of the London Motor Cab Company of Chelsea at a rank in the Strand. Because of the shape of its body, the Rational was nicknamed the 'pillar box cab'. It was made in Hertfordshire by Heatly-Gresham Engineering. One was hired by a journalist for a trip from Northumberland Avenue to Brighton, which took three and a half hours.

There was a minimum height between the seat cushion and the roof of not less than 40 inches to allow a gentleman to sit while wearing a top hat. (This is still possible in the latest cabs.) The front edges of the cushions in a four-seat cab should not be less than 19 inches apart, to ensure that a lady and a gentleman sitting opposite each other would not find their knees touching.

Despite the protest, there was a boom in the number and variety of cabs built to comply with the new rules. Some, like the Dawfield-Phillips and the Pullcar, were produced in small numbers, whilst Mann & Overton's sold the Unic 10/12 hp by the hundreds. Many fleets bought them, including the City & Suburban Cab Company and also the National Cab Company of Hammersmith, who employed young W. O. Bentley as a manager. Fiat set up its own cab company, with four hundred cabs, whereas a similar attempt by Rover foundered. Another casualty was the Automobile Cab Company, which

Left: The Vauxhall hansom cab. It was said to be popular with cabmen, although the remote controls would have made it feel very vague to drive. Most passengers found this cab alarming: 'The apparent rushing straight into danger without seeing that the driver is doing anything to avert it must be at times disconcerting,' said the *Commercial Motor*.

Middle: A Herald of the Metropolitan Cab and Carriage Company, photographed at New Scotland Yard. The driver is believed to be Mr Hinkley, the first cabman to hold a motor cab licence. The policeman in the cap is Chief Inspector Arthur Bassom, the head of the Public Carriage Office. The man on the left of the picture is Sergeant Hicks.

Below: The Unic 10/12 was introduced by Mann & Overton in 1905. The seat beside the cabman was outlawed in 1907. The Public Carriage Office's Chief Inspector Bassom maintained that the space beside the cabman was 'not suitable for a seat, but might be useful for ladies' shopping or to put small parcels on'.

in 1905 had ordered two hundred Model 'B' Fords, but Henry Ford refused to adapt the chassis for the Conditions of Fitness and, when threatened with legal action by the Automobile Cab Company, told them 'Fire away!'. Meanwhile the Automobile Cab Company ordered forty French Sorexes, but they were out of business by 1910. Many other makes were introduced, with varying degrees of success, such as Argyll, Adams, Darracq, Electromobile, Albion, Charron, Hillman-Coatelen, Austin, Lotis, Belsize, Ballot, Wolseley-Siddeley and Humber. Two successful makes were Panhard and Napier, operated by the firm of W. & G. du Cros of Acton, whose fleet, at its height, exceeded a thousand cabs. In 1910 Mann & Overton's contracted with Unic to produce a new model, the 12/16 hp, which was specifically designed to meet the Conditions of Fitness. Its reliability and economy made it a great success, ensuring that Mann & Overton's became the most prominent cab dealer in London.

Unlike private hire, the taxi trade in the United Kingdom is not allowed to set its own fares. Taxicab fares have always been set by the relevant licensing authority, in London's case the government through the Home Office. At this time, motor cabs had charged the same tariff as horse cabs, but some cab companies began fitting taximeters, which the PCO allowed, but often they registered fares higher than those permitted, a practice which the PCO had no powers to ban until, on 1 July 1907, the fitting of taximeters became mandatory and regulations were framed for them. They were sealed to prevent tampering, but this did not prevent anyone trying. Once meters became mandatory, garages charged their drivers a percentage of the total meter readings instead of a daily rate, as was horse-cab practice, but

Mann & Overton's Ltd was formed in 1898 by John James Mann and Tom Overton. No other company has had as great an influence on the London cab trade as 'M & O'.

UNIC CABS

12/16 H.P. UNIC Cab Chassis
without Tyres
£295.

12/16 H.P. UNIC Cab,
Complete,
£405.

Telephone 4634 Victoria.
Telegrams
"Soupape-Sloane, London."

12/16 H.P. UNIC TAXI-CAB.

MANN & OVERTON'S, Ltd., 10, Lower Grosvenor Place, London.
57, Whitworth Street West, Manchester.

Unic 12/16s in a cab garage somewhere in London. Edwardian cabmen kept their cabs gleaming.

W. O. Bentley's employers, the National Cab Company, found that they were unaccountably losing money. After a long investigation, Bentley found that some cabmen had drilled minute holes in the glass of the meters and by inserting a pin through it they were able to turn the mechanism back to a lower reading and thus were liable to pay less money to the company!

Along with the ruling, a new tariff was set for motor cabs. The hiring charge was 8d (3.3p), rather than the one shilling (5p) applicable to horse cabs to compensate for the waiting time automatically recorded by the taximeter while the cab was standing still. The new tariff gave rise to a popular song, 'You can do it in style for eight pence a mile', but this tariff was not liked by the proprietors, as they had based their costs on horse-cab fares and they were losing money. This was aggravated by the refusal of the then Home Secretary, Winston Churchill, to grant a fare increase.

A two-cylinder Renault AG. The purchase of five hundred by the General Cab Company caused controversy, as the cab did not comply with the Conditions of Fitness. However, the company was set up in 1905 and the cab may have been approved before the rules were in force. Inspector Bassom was said to have allowed them to operate 'in the public interest'.

Motor cabs were at first permitted to carry a third passenger beside the cabman, but under the London Cab and Stage Carriage Act of 1907 this practice became illegal. Inspector Bassom felt that some individuals might interfere with the cab's controls and cause an accident. From then on, the two-seat cab would be phased out, particularly as one feature of London cab fares had been carried over from horse cabs: the 'extras'. These included a 2d (0.8p) charge for every additional passenger more than two. The cabmen considered the extras theirs, as horse cabmen did, because horse cabs carried no meter to register them. But the companies also wanted them, to try to remain profitable. In 1911 the London Cab Drivers' Trade Union called a strike of cabmen, demanding to keep the extras, and they won. Cabmen had to pay for their own fuel, but when, in late 1912, the cost rose to one shilling a gallon, cabmen struck for subsidised petrol. After a prolonged and acrimonious dispute, they won again, but it signalled the end of most of the big fleets, as they could no longer make profit. Fiat gave up. W. & G. du Cros cut its fleet down, converting many of its cabs into delivery vans. The General Cab Company survived, but in 1908 it had merged with the United Motor Cab Company from west London to form the London General Cab Company. Many proprietors sold their cabs off to cabmen, and so London would have a far higher proportion of owner-drivers than most of the world's cities. The main beneficiary was Mann & Overton's, which continued to sell the Unic to fleet proprietors and owner-drivers alike. By 1914 the Unic was the only cab available on the London market.

By the outbreak of the First World War, the number of hansoms had shrunk from 5,923 in 1907 to just 232. The growler, because of its luggage capacity, had clung to working the railway termini, but by 1914 there were just 1,159 left out of the 3,924 that were around in 1904. By contrast, the number of motor cabs had grown in the same decade from three to 7,260.

Below left: 'The smartest in the land!' proclaimed the man who sent the postcard from which this picture was taken. The cab is a four-cylinder 15 hp Napier, operated by W. & G. du Cros of Acton.

Below right: A taximeter of the Edwardian pattern. When the 'flag' was up, the cab was for hire. When the cab was hired, the cabman swung it downwards to set the meter in operation. A small lamp was provided to enable the passengers to see the recorded fare at night.

KOSMOS TAXAMETERS

Specially adapted for OWNER DRIVERS, and for such is undoubtedly the best Taxameter on the Market.

LARGELY USED IN LONDON AND ALL PROVINCIAL TOWNS.

Special terms to OWNER DRIVERS.

Apply to . .

The Premier Taxameter Co., Ltd.,

106, ALBANY STREET, LONDON, N.W.

This advert is from Mann and Overton's *Motor Atlas* of 1914. From 1913, the number of owner-drivers in London grew as the big fleets declined. Since the days of horse cabs, owner-drivers had been known as 'Mushes', as they seemed to spring up like mushrooms and, in those times disappear just as quickly.

FARES

For Motor Hackney Carriages fitted with a TAXIMETER.

(a) Not exceeding One Mile, or for a Period of Time (waiting) or Journey, of Ten Minutes - - - - — 8d.

(b) Exceeding One Mile or Ten Minutes—

(1) For each Quarter-Mile, Period of Time (waiting) or Journey, of Two and Half-Minutes - - — 2d.

(2) For any less period or distance - - - - - — 2d.

EXTRA PAYMENTS.

WHETHER HIRED BY DISTANCE OR BY TIME—

(1) Luggage—

For each Package carried outside (Luggage carried on the footboard so that the doors do not close over it is deemed to be outside) - - - - - - - - - - - — 2d.

(2) Extra Persons—

For each additional PERSON beyond TWO the whole journey (Two Children under Ten Years of age count as One Person) - — 6d.

(This only applies to Cabs licensed to carry more than Two Persons).

Any complaints respecting defective Taximeters should be at once made to the Public Carriage Office, New Scotland Yard, or at any Police Station.

A fare table for a four-seat taxicab. These were posted inside the cab for the passenger's information.

MC1000
THE
MORRIS-COMMERCIA
INTERNATIONAL
TAXI-CAB

KOSMOS TAXAMETERS

Specially adapted for OWNER DRIVERS, and for such is undoubtedly the best Taxameter on the Market.

LARGELY USED IN LONDON AND ALL PROVINCIAL TOWNS.

Special terms to OWNER DRIVERS.

Apply to . .

The Premier Taxameter Co., Ltd.,
106, ALBANY STREET, LONDON, N.W.

This advert is from Mann and Overton's *Motor Atlas* of 1914. From 1913, the number of owner-drivers in London grew as the big fleets declined. Since the days of horse cabs, owner-drivers had been known as 'Mushes', as they seemed to spring up like mushrooms and, in those times disappear just as quickly.

FARES

For Motor Hackney Carriages fitted with a TAXIMETER.

(a) Not exceeding One Mile, or for a Period of Time (waiting) or Journey, of Ten Minutes - - - — 8d.

(b) Exceeding One Mile or Ten Minutes—

(1) For each Quarter-Mile, Period of Time (waiting) or Journey, of Two and Half-Minutes - - — 2d.

(2) For any less period or distance - - - - - — 2d.

EXTRA PAYMENTS.

WHETHER HIRED BY DISTANCE OR BY TIME—

(1) Luggage—

For each Package carried outside (Luggage carried on the footboard so that the doors do not close over it is deemed to be outside) - - - - - - - - - - — 2d.

(2) Extra Persons—

For each additional PERSON beyond TWO the whole journey (Two Children under Ten Years of age count as One Person) - — 6d.

(This only applies to Cabs licensed to carry more than Two Persons).

Any complaints respecting defective Taximeters should be at once made to the Public Carriage Office, New Scotland Yard, or at any Police Station.

A fare table for a four-seat taxicab. These were posted inside the cab for the passenger's information.

MC1000
THE
MORRIS-COMMERCIA
INTERNATIONAL
TAXI-CAB

THE 1920s

AFTER the First World War there were fewer than 2,400 cabs still serviceable. At first, cabmen who had fought in the war and hoped to return to work struggled to find a fleet proprietor who had a cab available, or, if they had money, they were unable to afford to buy those cabs that were for sale, but soon an aspiring owner-driver could buy a second-hand two-cylinder Renault for £200 on hire purchase, or £180 cash.

In May 1919 the first post-war taxicab was announced, from William Beardmore & Company Ltd, a huge Scottish engineering concern, with interests in shipbuilding, iron, steel and aero engines. Its owner, Sir William Beardmore, was the largest shareholder in Arrol-Johnston cars, and the Beardmore taxicab originated in Arrol-Johnston's old factory in Paisley, near Glasgow, in 1915, although its development had been halted when the war escalated. It was purpose-built in co-operation with the Public Carriage Office to comply with the Conditions of Fitness, which had remained unchanged since 1906. Although it was expensive at £625, its superior quality earned it the title of 'the Rolls-Royce of taxicabs'. This model was replaced by a much-modified Mark II 'Super' in 1923. This was built on a chassis derived from Beardmore's new light commercial vehicle and it too proved very popular. By the end of the 1920s, Beardmore claimed that it had made half the cabs running in London.

By contrast, its contemporary the Mepward was dreadful. Too heavy for its engine, it was very slow and soon disappeared. Other makes, such as AML, Kingsway, Fiat and Darracq, never went into production, but Mann & Overton's was soon able to import a revised version of the pre-war 12/16 Unic and sold it from its new premises in Battersea Bridge Road for £625.

Dyer & Holton provided the body for the Unic and another newcomer, the 11.4 hp Citroën, designed and sold by west London dealers Maxwell Monson in 1923. At £540, it was cheaper than the Beardmore or the Unic, but it could be had with a full electric lighting set, an extra not universally liked by cabmen, as the lights drained the battery too quickly. Besides, the PCO frowned upon bright headlights, as they might dazzle other road users. One of the biggest buyers of Citroën cabs was the London General Cab Company.

Opposite: The leading illustration from the catalogue for the first Morris-Commercial cab. A very popular vehicle, it was robust and comparatively inexpensive to buy.

The MkI Beardmore appeared in 1919. Built in Paisley, near Glasgow, the cabs were tested rigorously on the hilly roads around Loch Lomond. The frame was dropped halfway along, in order to give a reasonably low entrance and yet still comply with the 10 inch ground clearance demanded by the Conditions of Fitness. Most Beardmore MkIs were finished in a standard dark green colour.

W. & G. du Cros, operating cabs in much reduced circumstances as the Turpin Engineering Company, imported a modified version of the American Yellow Cab in 1923, but this was short-lived, as was another make with transatlantic origins, the Hayes, which used a Canadian-built chassis. It was sold by Liverpool-based Morris dealer William Watson.

But the cab trade was operating in troubled times, and not only because of the country's economic stagnation. In 1925 the vain and unlikeable Home Secretary, Sir William Joynson-Hicks – 'Jix' to his colleagues – appointed a committee to hear evidence on the question of two-seat cabs for London. The proponents claimed that a four-seat cab could not be run profitably at less than the current one shilling per mile, which they said was too high a tariff. Certainly cheap bus, tram and tube fares had taken a lot of work from the cab trade. A two-seater cab, they said, would be cheap to buy and could be run profitably at 9d a mile. The cab trade was unanimously against the two-seater, arguing that there were already too many taxis on the streets working for only three hours out of a twelve-hour shift; more cabs would only make matters worse. The committee eventually came out cautiously in favour of the two-seater. In a splendidly roundabout way, they said that 'It is not desirable that the Home Secretary should make an order which would prohibit the licensing of a vehicle which complies with Scotland Yard requirements on the sole grounds that it is constructed to carry fewer than four passengers'. Joynson-Hicks licensed them in April 1926 under the Two-Seater Order. The press called these new cabs 'Jixis', after the Home Secretary's nickname, but only three prototypes, the KRC, the Berliet and the Trojan, appeared. A year later Jix rescinded the Two-Seater Order but nevertheless cut fares from one shilling to 9d per mile.

In the following year, 1927, 'Jix' did what he ought to have done in 1925 and instigated a review of the Conditions of Fitness. By now, only the Beardmore Mk2 was available. The Citroën, Hayes and Unic were gone and the progress of car design had left the regulations way behind. The head of the PCO, Arthur Bassom, now Superintendent, had been put in charge of

11.4 hp Citroën, illustrated by some stylised artwork. This cab was unusual in having Michelin disc wheels. The cab's leading semi-elliptical front springs sometimes caused serious vibration in the axle when driven over cobblestones.

the Metropolitan Police's new Traffic Division and had been concentrating on police aviation, but he had died in 1926, aged sixty-one, never having presided over a major review of his own regulations. Now it was proving even more difficult to produce a vehicle to meet them.

A technical committee was set up under Captain Douglas Hacking, the Parliamentary Secretary of State at the Home Office, who invited several members of the motor industry to attend. Only Humber and Morris bothered to send representatives, both of whom said that the Conditions of Fitness were too strict for them to make a cab at a realistic price. In reaching its conclusion, the committee condemned the Home Secretary for the 'Jixi' fiasco and the lack of care given by the government to the London cab trade. They recommended that the turning circle be enlarged to 40 feet, the ground clearance be reduced to 7 inches and that advertisements should be

In response to the revised Conditions of Fitness, the London General Cab Company built an exclusive model of Citroën cab, using the new 13/30 engine and the old Dyer & Holton bodies, stretched in front of the partition to fit the longer wheelbase. Note the new smaller 20 inch diameter wheels and balloon tyres.

Right: a Mk 2 Beardmore 'Super'. Although it used a similar engine and gearbox to the Mk 1, almost everything else about it was new.

Above: As well as issuing a licence plate, the PCO would apply a stencil, bearing the initials of the Commissioner of the Metropolitan Police to the nearside rear of the cab. The design was changed each year. This prevented a plate being fitted to a vehicle that had not been inspected and passed.

permitted inside cabs, but not outside. However, Bassom's successor, Spt. Claro, argued in favour of the tight turning circle and it was retained.

Now it was possible for more manufacturers to enter the market. But, even before the new regulations were in force, a new cab appeared from Morris-Commercial, the G-Type International. It was promoted by the Leeds Morris dealer George Kenning. It would be sold by the man who introduced the Hayes, William Watson. Solid and stately, it gained a fine reputation, with over 1,700 being sold by the time it was replaced in 1932.

The Morris-Commercial G-Type International was made at Soho, Birmingham. The body is a three-quarter landaulette type, distinguished by the extra side window. The cab got its 'International' tag not from any anticipated exports but from its sponsor, Leeds Morris dealer George Kenning, who owned the International Cab Company.

The 'Cape' body, shown on the right, was the idea of a South African businessman, W. Gowan, and named after his home city, Cape Town. It had sliding doors but left the cabman in a very exposed position. This is the first, on a Morris-Commercial G-Type chassis, alongside a Citroën. Some were later fitted to Austin 12/4 chassis but they were never popular.

The first cab to comply with the new regulations was the Mk3 'Hyper' Beardmore, based on the chassis of the defunct 12/30 Beardmore car. At £425, it was substantially cheaper than the Mk2 and was the first London cab to feature four-wheel brakes. Previously, such items had been forbidden by the PCO as it considered they would encourage furious driving!

In 1929 the London General Cab Company brought out its own Citroën-based cab, designed and built at its works and fitted with the bodies from retired 11.4 hp cabs. A new design of body with fixed head was designed in house, and around eighty were made. However, 'The General' soon had its eyes on a new and much better vehicle: the Austin 12/4.

The Mk3 Beardmore 'Hyper' introduced in 1928, was a radical departure from the massive Mk1 and Mk2 that preceded it. Based on the defunct Beardmore 12/30 private-car chassis, the Hyper was the last model to be

Austin
LOW LOADING
TAXI-CAB
TAXI
Austin
MO 1938

THE 1930s

TAXICAB regulations in the United Kingdom outside London have always been framed by individual local authorities within set parameters, allowing a wide variety of vehicles to be licensed to suit local needs. Mann & Overton's had had premises in Manchester since before the First World War and had been selling the Austin 12/4 as a cab there, where its price, reliability and serviceability had made it very popular. Will Overton, now in charge of Mann & Overton's, believed that the Austin's chassis could be adapted to meet the new Conditions of Fitness and persuaded Herbert Austin to supply him with an initial order for five hundred suitably modified chassis.

The first model, the HL, was introduced in 1929 and was christened by the cab trade the 'High Lot'. Morris and Beardmore supplied their cabs complete with a body but Austin, despite having an extensive body department of its own, would not supply cab bodies, so Mann & Overton's signed up a selection of approved coachbuilders. The first 12/4 cabs were fitted with landaulette bodies by Dyer & Holton of Brixton, the Chelsea Carriage Company and Christopher Dodson of Chelsea. The last two did not continue supplying, but bodies by Strachan (pronounced 'Strawn') of Acton, Jones of Westbourne Grove and Vincents of Reading were offered in the catalogue. Priced at £395, the HL proved very popular from the outset and by the end of 1932 more than seven hundred had been sold. A revised Austin, the TT, appeared in 1933, with a new gearbox. During 1933, an impressive 834 TTs were sold, demonstrating that the Austin 12/4 was the cab the trade had yearned for – cheap to buy, economical to run and thoroughly reliable. Austin set aside part of its advertising budget to cab development, as the sight of its vehicles doing one of the toughest jobs in the nation was a superb advertisement for them. There were still a huge number of elderly cabs on the road, some dating from before the First World War, and because of the success of the Austin the Public Carriage Office issued a directive that any cab over fifteen years old would no longer be licensed unless it was in exceptional condition.

Mann & Overton's had relinquished the concession for Unic cars and trucks, which was picked up by Ernest Mepstead, the 'Mep' of Mepward. (The other

Opposite: Mann & Overton's brochure for the Austin 12/4 'Low Loading' taxicab.

Vincents of Reading was one of the standard body suppliers for Austin cabs. This HL from 1930, carrying a Vincents full Landaulette body, is one of the oldest surviving examples of the marque.

King's Cross station rank in the early 1930s: 'on point' is a Mk1 Beardmore. Behind is an Austin (either an HL or a TT) with a Jones three-quarter landaulette body, and the third cab is a Mk2 Beardmore 'Super'. The drivers of the front two cabs on a rank are required by law to stay with their cabs at all times.

half, Hayward, was reputed to be languishing in prison.) In 1929 Mepstead bought cab chassis based on Unic's current car, adapted to meet the revised Conditions of Fitness. Fitted with a choice of bodies by Jones Brothers or Goode & Cooper, they were not reliable cabs and only about a hundred were made.

Beardmore Motors was on the move. The whole of Beardmore's Clydeside empire had collapsed in the 1920s and in 1932 the directors of Beardmore Motors bought the company and moved production to their premises in Hendon, north London. Here they produced the last of the Hypers and, with the assistance of Jack Irving, designer of Captain Henry Segrave's land speed record cars and now employed by the Rootes Group, designed a new model, the MkIV 'Paramount', using the new Commer van engine. Although this cab was supplied with a high-quality body by Beardmore's neighbours, Windovers, Beardmore's production capacity was much reduced and the Paramount's price was £450, so Beardmore never recovered its dominance of the trade.

Morris-Commercial replaced the G-Type in 1932 with a new model, the G2, which became known as the 'Junior' because it was noticeably smaller than the high and mighty G-Type.

In 1934 Austin produced a new cab chassis, the LL ('Low Loading') cab, which was, as the name suggests, much lower than the HL, as the revised 7-inch ground clearance had now been done away with, along with the 14-foot maximum length. Standard bodies were supplied for the LL by Vincents and Strachan, whilst a Jones body was £5 extra. The 'Low Loader', as it became universally known, was a massive success; in four years, Mann & Overton's sold more than 3,800 to a trade that ran fewer than seven thousand vehicles, leaving Beardmore and Morris-Commercial way behind. Mann & Overton (they dropped the possessive *'s* in 1935) were firmly back on top.

The MkIV Beardmore Paramount was the first model to be built at Hendon. It was available as a full or three-quarter landaulette or as a saloon body. The full landaulette body style was favoured by night men for the discretion it offered a certain type of female passengers and their clientele. Such jobs could prove quite lucrative.

The Austin 12/4 LL proved to be the most popular cab during the 1930s. The body by Jones shown here featured curled ends to the roof racks.

The next Morris-Commercial cab, the G2S of 1935, was powered by a six-cylinder engine, the first in a London cab, and was nicknamed the 'Junior Six'. The cab was powerful, but the trade did not appreciate the extra two cylinders, as they meant extra maintenance at a time when engines needed far more than today. The Morris-Commercial cabs were also said to be heavy to drive. Both these factors restricted sales, despite a price of £385, £10 cheaper than the Austin.

In 1936 Beardmore produced a new model, the MkV Paramount Ace. This had a longer chassis, which gave the passengers a more comfortable ride, and a new gearbox. The Beardmore was fast and good to drive and its nickname was 'the greengrocer's barrow' (because all the best things were in front!) but, owing to Beardmore's limited production capacity and the cab's high price of £485, it sold only in small numbers.

In late 1938 the last new models before the outbreak of war appeared. Austin's new model was the FL, which carried a new radiator shell and wings similar to those of Austin's contemporary private cars. This 'streamlined' look earned it the nickname of 'Flash Lot'. A new feature was a full-height driver's

The G2SW was the last Morris-Commercial cab made before the Second World War. As well as having a window in the driver's door, it featured a petrol gauge, something the Austin did not have. Austin owners were provided with a graduated wooden stick to check their fuel reserves.

Above: The MkV Beardmore Paramount Ace was built on a new, longer chassis, seating the passengers ahead of the rear axle. The similar MkVI Ace was the first London cab to have a one-piece windscreen, although like all taxicab windscreens it was required to open to allow good visibility in the capital's 'pea souper' fogs.

door with a window, giving the cabman some protection from side winds and rain. The new Morris-Commercial G25W also had this luxury, plus a new overhead-valve six-cylinder engine. Beardmore's MkVI Ace had glass in the driver's door and, for the first time in a London cab, a one-piece windscreen.

As war loomed, Morris-Commercial cab dealer William Watson decided to retire. The Nuffield organisation, Morris-Commercial's parent company, had decided to develop a new model at the Wolseley factory in Birmingham. Fitted with a Jones landaulette body, it was put on trial by Beardmore Motors, who had agreed to take over the dealership of Nuffield cabs upon Watson's retirement.

Although cabs were proportionately cheaper than they were in the 1920s, private cars had become cheaper still and the Hindley Report, published in 1939, sought to find if a cheaper cab, at perhaps £330 and with a shorter life, could be made. However, the war that had been expected for three or more years became a reality in September 1939, and the Hindley Report was not acted upon.

Below left: The Austin 12/4 FL, or 'Flash Lot', with a Strachan body. The FL gave the cabman a little more comfort, with its driver's door window.

Below right: A cabman's and passenger's eye view of the taximeter in the 1930s. The type of meter changed little between the wars. Note the lamp, demanded by the PCO to enable the passengers to read the fare at night.

THE SECOND WORLD WAR

Anti-aircraft fire, Home Guard style, from the 59th County of London (Taxi) Battalion. Although cabmen have always been notoriously difficult to organise, the Home Guard Battalion was said to have responded well to Army discipline. The cab is a 1935 Austin LL with a Jones body.

BEARDMORE had agreed to take on the dealership of Nuffield cabs, so it ceased production of its own MkVI before the declaration of war and turned its factory over to the production of munitions. Beardmore Motors ran the Nuffield prototype cab throughout the war. Driven by Roy Perkins, who had failed his medical when called up, it covered 300,000 miles and was regularly inspected by senior men from Wolseley, who had made the cab. A few Austins were delivered up to January 1940, and about four hundred chassis with light truck bodies were acquired by the Army, which used them for general duties and driving instruction.

Taxicabs and their drivers played an important part in the defence of London between 1939 and 1945. When war was declared, their strength stood at 6,690 motor cabs. There were also eight growlers and one hansom, the fate of which is not known, but the last hansom driver turned in his licence in 1947.

As early as 1938, an Act of Parliament allowed the formation of the Auxiliary Fire Service (AFS) and 2,800 fire-pump trailers were commissioned by the Home Office. The Cab Trade Committee of the Transport and General Workers Union suggested requisitioning London cabs to tow some of them, and recruiting cabmen to drive them, because if a road became impassable a cabman would know the best way round to get to the blaze. Every cab owned by a fleet was earmarked for towing trailer-mounted fire pumps and, at the outbreak of war, all requisitioned cabmen were called up and began training. However, the Austin 12/4 was not powerful enough to haul the trailer and to carry ladders on its roof, hoses in the luggage compartment and five crewmen in hilly areas,

and many were returned to their owners; the task was carried out by large saloon cars and purpose-built fire appliances. Nevertheless, just over two thousand cabs were retained, and their drivers, at first derided as men who were dodging the call-up, performed the most heroic feats in the Blitz. Churchill called AFS crew members 'heroes with dirty faces'.

Working cabmen found driving difficult in the blackout. There was a 20 mph speed limit, but cabmen were forbidden to use their dashboard lights to illuminate the speedometer. However, they were allowed to switch on the light at brief intervals to check their speed. One cabman who did this and bent down to peer at the speedometer ran over a policeman who was trying to stop him for exceeding the speed limit!

Above: The London Fire Brigade mostly chose Strachan-bodied Austins such as this 1935 example so as to standardise on towing brackets. This is an early picture; although the cab has blackout markings and headlight masks, it has yet to be painted in the standard Auxiliary Fire Service grey.

A small number of cabs were used as passenger ambulances. Other cabs were requisitioned by the 59th County of London (Taxi) Battalion, the Home Guard, along with their drivers, who were retained, as a memorandum in the *Motor Cab Owner Drivers' Gazette* said, 'for the sole purpose of driving (or maintaining) taxicabs according to the declaration made upon their Enrolment Forms'.

For the first and only time in its history, Mann & Overton rented cabs out, rather than just selling and servicing them. Despite heroic efforts by the company to keep war-worn cabs on the road, even making some spare parts itself, many taxis were off the road because of a lack of spares. Others had been destroyed in air raids. In 1945 there were fewer than three thousand cabs fit for use.

Left: The 59th County of London (Taxi) Battalion of the Home Guard on manoeuvres. To judge by the different vehicles on parade, 'Dad's Army' was less selective about the types of cab it requisitioned than was the AFS.

THE 1940s AND 1950s

WITH the Oxford, Nuffield had a head start over Austin. They worked flat out to get the cab introduced by late 1947, in time to be used for the transport of the guests at the wedding of Princess Elizabeth to Prince Philip Mountbatten, an occasion that brought glamour and style to the bleak post-war years. The Public Carriage Office had decided that post-war cabs should be more like modern cars, although retaining some distinct difference, and thus had banned landaulette bodies: the Oxford, therefore, had a fixed-head body, panelled in pressed steel. But it was expensive, at almost £1,000, including the 33⅓ per cent purchase tax levied on luxury goods, large cars and taxicabs, and so sales were very slow in a city where few people had spare cash to spend. The situation was greatly hindered by fares remaining at the tariff set in 1933. Cab proprietors were obliged to keep their pre-war cabs running, and the PCO had to suspend the fifteen-year rule, imposed in 1933.

Austin provided Mann & Overton with a new chassis, the FX, in late 1945, powered by a side-valve engine. Mann & Overton tested it, fitted with a landaulette body, but it proved inadequate, and so Austin designed a new one, the FX2, which was ready in 1947. Austin had designed an all-steel fixed-head body, but was not able to make it, and so introduced Mann & Overton to Carbodies Ltd, a Coventry coachbuilder who had made aircraft components for Austin during the war. Carbodies agreed to build the cab and supply one quarter of the finance, along with another quarter from Austin and a half from Mann & Overton. However, Austin scrapped the side-valve engine in favour of a new overhead-valve engine. The final prototype, the FX3, with its pressed-steel body and new engine, began tests in June 1948 and went on sale the following November. Like the Oxford, it was expensive. To compound the problems, double purchase tax was levied in 1951, putting up the price of cabs to over £1,100.

The FX3 was further handicapped by a fuel consumption of 18 miles per gallon (mpg), compared with 25 mpg of the 12/4. North London cab and coach proprietor John Birch tried the Standard Motor Company's new small diesel engine in one of his FX3s and it returned 38 mpg. A bonus was that

Opposite: From the Series III Nuffield Oxford brochure, this evocative 1950s artwork promotes the two versions of the vehicle: taxicab (top) and the four-door hire car.

Right: A Series I Oxford, pictured in the snow in late 1947 near Regent's Park, not far from Beardmore Motors' showrooms in Great Portland Street, from where it was sold.

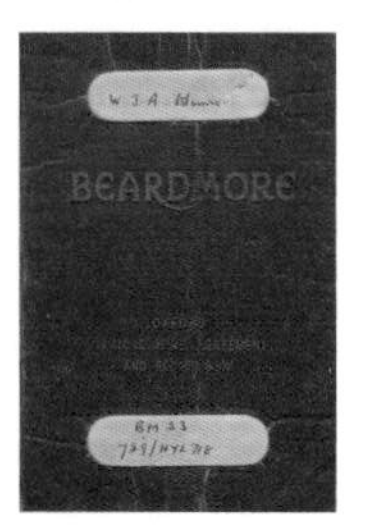

Above: A payments book for a Series I Oxford, dating from 1949. It was issued by Beardmore Motors, which sold the Oxford. Weekly payments of £3 11s 6d (£3.57½) were made in person, in cash, over four years at Beardmore's sales office in Great Portland Street.

diesel fuel then was a fraction of the price of petrol. Birch offered the conversion to the trade and it proved very popular. A Perkins and a Borgward diesel were tried too, in both the Austin and the Oxford, but Mann & Overton was opposed to this practice and persuaded Austin to produce a diesel engine of its own. It was introduced in 1954 and, although costing an additional £85 plus tax, it soon outsold the petrol model by nine to one. Austin would benefit in 1953 by the complete removal of purchase tax on cabs, bringing the price down to an affordable level. This, along with a slight increase in work and a higher tariff, meant that the trade slowly began to prosper and the pre-war cabs could now be taken off the road.

Right: The FX2 prototype, with a coachbuilt body, photographed by Carbodies' managing director, Ernest Jones. Hub caps were not permitted at first, to enable carriage officers to see if all the wheel nuts were in place.

The first Austin FX3 brochure shows the cab to be a luxurious vehicle, conveying the passenger in style. Note the hubcaps, which were permitted soon after the cab's introduction.

A four-door hire-car version of the FX3, the FL1, was made, finding use in the private hire trade, in ambulance work and as the base for a hearse. The FX3 chassis was also fitted with van bodies, including some that were used to deliver London evening newspapers.

The FX3 was the first London taxicab to be exported in any quantity. Foreign sales numbered about seven hundred, of which 250 went to Spain and the balance to Sweden, Denmark, Ireland, Iran and New Zealand. One was tried in New York, others in San Francisco and in Boston and other cities on the east coast of the United States, but they were underpowered compared with the American cabs, and the tight turning circle was of no advantage in cities with wide avenues. The high purchase price was not appreciated: London proprietors paid a high purchase price and expected a ten-year life, whereas American cab companies bought cheaper standard saloon cars and ran them for just a few years.

The changes in motor industry practice established a tradition in the London cab trade. There has never been a law decreeing that London cabs should be black. Pre-war cabs were seen in different colours, but the Oxford and the FX3 were produced in a standard black, with alternative colours available at extra cost. Proprietors knew that a cab of a different colour did

Right: KGT 756 is the oldest Austin FX3 known to survive. It is over-painted in Lansdowne maroon, to commemorate the coronation of Queen Elizabeth II in June 1953.

Above: The stencil from KGT 756, dating from 1954. The initials are of Police Commissioner Sir John Nott-Bower. Note the new style of crown compared to the stencil on page 21. It is that of Queen Elizabeth II.

not earn them any more money than a black one, so in the difficult economic climate black became the standard colour for London taxicabs. Indeed, all the pre-war cabs still running were painted black so as to blend in.

Production of the Oxford ended in 1953. When Austin and Nuffield combined to form the British Motor Corporation in 1952, Beardmore Motors was given a year's notice that the Oxford was to be scrapped. Beardmore then decided to return to taxi making, designing a traditional-style cab, the Mk7, using a coachbuilt body by Windovers. Its aluminium panels made the cab very light and enabled Beardmore to use Ford's modest-

Above: An early Austin FX3, this time with hub caps, and trafficators. The FX3 was described as being an 'enclosed drive' cab; it was the first to have a sliding glass partition beside the driver. The Oxford was intended to have this from the outset, but lack of money prevented its fitting until later.

The Series III Oxford could be distinguished by its 'Easiclean' pressed-steel wheels and an extra side window.

Undoubtedly the most distinctive body mounted on an FX3 chassis was that commissioned by the flamboyant Armenian oil magnate Nubar Gulbenkian, who lived in London. When asked why he chose a taxi for his personal transport, he replied: 'because it can turn on a sixpence; whatever that may be.'

sized Consul engine. It was introduced at the end of 1954 but sold only in limited numbers, partly because of Beardmore's limited production facility and partly because the fleet proprietors preferred the Austin's steel body, which could be repaired more quickly and easily. In 1958 Windovers was bought by Weymann, the bus builder, and production of Beardmore cabs was transferred to the Weymann factory in Addlestone, Surrey.

John Birch went much further than fitting new engines in cabs. He designed his own cab, based on a Standard Vanguard chassis and powered by the Standard diesel. Of a modern style, it was unconventional in using a seating arrangement occasionally used in the United States for taxis of saloon-car type, where three passengers sat on the rear seat and a fourth in a fixed,

This gentleman, a Mr A. J. Skinner from Camberwell, is the lucky winner of a brand new Mk7 Beardmore, which he collected from the Hendon works.

rear-facing seat beside the driver, separated by a dog-leg partition. Luggage was carried in a separate compartment at the rear. It was approved in December 1955 but only the one was built and changes within the Standard Motor Company prevented further development.

In 1958 the Austin FX3 was replaced by an entirely new model, the FX4, the first production four-door cab to be licensed in London. Like the FX3, it was made on behalf of Mann & Overton by Carbodies using Austin mechanical components. It was also financed through the same three-way

The revolutionary Birch cab, styled like a contemporary Standard Ten. Note the absence of a nearside front door, the luggage being carried in a rear compartment. The body was built by Park Royal Vehicles Ltd, which made many of the bodies for London Transport buses.

Vans based on the FX3 chassis were used by all three of London's evening newspapers. This one, used by the *Evening Standard*, was run by a sub-contractor, United. The state of the buildings behind the van shows how long London had to live with the destruction suffered during the Blitz.

arrangement, although there was a change at Carbodies, which had been bought by the BSA group in 1954. It used the FX3's diesel engine, with an automatic gearbox as standard (there was no option of a manual gearbox), independent front suspension and dual-circuit hydraulic brakes. On seeing it for the first time in June 1958, the trade condemned it as being too big and too expensive. Mann & Overton's chairman, Robert Overton, confided to his diary: 'What a headache this is going to be!'

It proved to be a much bigger headache than he had imagined. When first in service, the FX4's automatic gearbox was found to be incompatible with the engine and would soon fail. It was very noisy to drive, the body rusted badly, and rainwater would leak in. Austin was obliged to engineer a manual gearbox, and later a petrol engine was offered, mainly for the FL2 hire-car version. Despite its problems, the FX4 was the best option for the trade, being readily available through Mann & Overton, which could provide a reliable source of spare parts, an absolute necessity in keeping cabs on the road.

In 1959 the Public Carriage Office changed the style of licence plate it issued. The 'year' stencils had gone, to be replaced with this type, which indicated the month the plate was issued within the numbering system. This number begins with 7, indicating it was issued in July, the seventh month. A smaller plate was fixed inside the cab for the information of the passengers, should there be any reason for them to complain about or praise the cabman.

A Swedish-made Halda taximeter of the type used in the 1950s. Taximeters had changed little since pre-war days but had gained internal lighting.

Austin
VJJ 754G

THE 1960s

When Prime Minister Harold Macmillan said in 1957 that Britain 'had never had it so good', he was right. The nation's economy was improving, and Londoners at last had money to spend. With the Austin FX4 dominant in a rising market, the Owner Drivers' Society decided it was time to invest in a new model of cab. They would call it the Winchester and it was scheduled for release in early 1961. It would be a step forward in design, using a complete fibreglass body.

John Birch, too, thought it was time for something new and went back to the Standard Motor Company. He acquired an example of the unloved and underpowered Atlas van, which he developed into a compact cab, but the Public Carriage Office disliked it at first sight and would not approve it. Beardmore, too, had been busy, working on a modern-shape Mk8, but this too was turned down by the PCO as top-heavy and ugly and also rejected by the London General Cab Company, whom Beardmore had been courting as a possible business partner. When Beardmore's management put it in their Great Portland Street showroom for the cab trade and the public to see, they realised what a mistake they had made with it.

But all three newcomers would be forced to put their projects on hold when, in 1961, the minicab arrived on the streets of London. It was the brainchild of Michael Gotla, a law graduate and proprietor of a private-hire company, Welbeck Motors. The cab trade, with fewer than seven thousand vehicles, could not keep up with the extra work and the PCO could not push cabmen fast enough through 'the Knowledge', the strict test that all would-be cab drivers have to undergo, to meet the demand. Gotla thought he could meet this demand by using a fleet of saloon cars and drivers that would ply for hire openly on the streets, just like taxis, using radios to make the advance bookings, supposedly to comply with the law. The cab trade was in uproar, with violence breaking out between cabmen and minicab drivers. Eventually, after protracted legal arguments, Gotla's way of working was deemed illegal, but rather than ban minicabs outright, as the cab trade demanded, the government instigated a new review of the Conditions of Fitness, to see if

Opposite: A 1967 Austin FX4, near a familiar London landmark.

Eric Bailey's artwork for the Austin FX4. It was this design that Mann & Overton's managing director, Robert Overton, liked best. Apart from the tail lights (and of course the colour), it differs little from the finished vehicle.

The first Austin FX4, photographed in Carbodies' car park. The door handles were inherited from the FX3 but proved too fragile on the new cab.

The first Austin FX4 to go into service was this one, VLW 431, which served as a test vehicle with York Way Motors from June 1958. It is photographed outside the gates of South Park, Fulham, close to Mann & Overton's premises.

One of the last FX3s to operate in London, photographed in Northumberland Avenue in the late 1960s. Note the new electro-mechanical taximeter. Because of the problems Carbodies had in delivering new FX4s, the Public Carriage Office was obliged to license some of the oldest FX3s for an eleventh year.

special vehicles were indeed necessary any more. Representatives of the trade put their case forcefully, and eventually, after over a year of deliberation, the committee decided in favour of maintaining the status quo. Now Winchester, Beardmore and Birch could begin again.

The Winchester was introduced in October 1962. Its fibreglass body was made by the long-established company of James Whitson & Sons. It had a Perkins diesel engine and was finished in two-tone grey with red vinyl upholstery. It was not liked by the trade, who found it uncomfortable, slow and very noisy to drive. Passengers were not happy with it either. It had what was described as an 'internal step', but some passengers did not see it, tripping over it and falling flat on their faces. Not for nothing was the Winchester given the nickname 'the pick 'em up and pull 'em out cab'!

Beardmore attempted a revised body for the Mk8, but it was too late, and it opted instead for a four-door version of the Mk7. A major strike at Weymann's factory in 1965 resulted in almost a year's production being lost and Weymann being taken over by Metropolitan-Cammell, forming Metropolitan-Cammell-Weymann (MCW). Cab production was then moved to Washwood Heath in Birmingham.

Meanwhile, Austin and Mann & Overton strengthened their hold on the market. Talks began on a replacement for the FX4, and Carbodies quoted £350,000 for a new body, which Mann & Overton thought too much. After discussions with sports-car

A police constable takes the particulars of one of A. Welbeck Motors' minicab driver. The police were rarely so keen to act over the flouting of the hackney carriage laws by minicab drivers, which caused a great deal of friction between police and taxi drivers.

After failing to produce a modern-style Mk8 cab, Beardmore added a fourth door to the Mk7. The body of this immaculately restored vehicle is by Weymann, which had made Beardmore's bodies since 1958.

makers Jensen and Gordon-Keeble about using a fibreglass body, they abandoned the idea and settled on a 'Mk2' version of the FX4, which addressed the complaints the trade had made about it. Soundproofing was added, cutting down on the incessant noise of the diesel engine. A new partition, which slid from side to side, was fitted, because the old one, which slid up and down, never stayed down after the cab was about five years old. The worst water leak, whereby rainwater would flood on to the driver's right foot, was cured by redesigning the battery trays, thereby doing away with the rust trap. The passenger heater, which was under the back seat and almost

The cover illustration from the first FX4 brochure.

Metropolitan-Cammell-Weymann's first Metrocab. The London General ran it for two years before deciding not to participate in its further development. The project was then shelved.

The Austin FX4 could be had in this 'driveaway' form, to enable outside body builders to fit different bodies. Some were used as 'gown vans' in the West End of London, while others were used as newspaper delivery vans. The FX4 chassis also served as the basis for a hearse.

The Austin FX4 was facelifted in late 1968. Missing are the separate sidelights, now incorporated into the headlights and roof-mounted 'limpet' indicators. The words 'FOR HIRE' in the roof light were too dim to be seen in daylight and were replaced by a better-illuminated yellow sign with the word 'TAXI'.

useless, was relocated behind the driver's seat. The roof-mounted limpet indicators, which were too high for average motorists to take notice of, were scrapped. They were replaced by the rear lights from BMC's Mk2 1100/1300 range. The new model was introduced in late 1967 and received a cautious welcome.

Winchester's fortunes, despite hard work, were not good. It was disappointed with James Whitson's work on the body and changed suppliers, to Wincanton Engineering. A new model, the Mk2, was the result, with the option of a Ford Cortina engine alongside the Perkins. The cab, introduced in 1965, was now finished in black. Two years later, Winchester lost its axle suppliers and went to Ford, which supplied Transit axles and a V4 petrol engine. Neither the Mk2 nor this new Mk3 sold well, with no more than about 120 made of the first three models.

Although Beardmore ceased trading as a company in 1969, some of its staff worked at MCW on a new cab, originally called the Metro-Beardmore, but, after several redesigns, a new prototype, the Metrocab, went into service

The Mk2 Winchester featured a Ford Cortina engine, as did the Brabham racing car into which the owner of the cab has been squeezed.

A Halda electro-mechanical taximeter from the 1960s. The key on the back face, to the right, sets the meter mode: 'for hire', 'hired' or stopped. When the cab is for hire, the words 'FOR HIRE' are illuminated. When the cab is hired, the small rectangular lamp on the front shows a green light.

with the London General. This light cab, powered by a Perkins 4.108 diesel, had a fibreglass body and a very modern shape. It was very economical to run, which pleased the General, but its very new design, something the trade had expected, actually worked against it. So used had the public become to the shape of the FX4 that they were reluctant to use the Metrocab, so the General hired it out to drivers at a much-reduced rate. After two years of working the cab, the General declined to finance its future development and so the project was shelved.

In the late 1960s Winchester brought out a new model, with an all-new body. This model, the Mk4, had Transit axles and a choice of a Ford Cortina petrol engine or a Perkins 4.108. A much better cab to drive, it came too late to save Winchester, and it was deleted in 1973, prior to the introduction of vehicle safety legislation that would come into force when Britain joined the European Common Market in January 1973.

The Perkins badge on the front of this Mk4 Winchester indicates that it is the diesel version. Fleet proprietor W. H. Cook converted some petrol versions to LPG (liquefied petroleum gas), claiming the £150 charge would be recouped within eight months. Cook also converted some petrol FX4s, but the whole project was wrecked by a large increase in the duty on LPG.

VICTORIA STATION
Brighton · Eastbourne · Gatwick
Worthing · Hove · Bognor Regis
BUSES ONLY SPEED LIMIT 4 M.P.H.
HOTELS
EJD 573V

THE 1970s AND 1980s

THE impending European vehicle regulations had two effects on the FX4. It had already benefited in late 1971 from a bigger, 2.5 litre engine but the petrol engine was now too dirty for the new exhaust emissions rules and was scrapped in 1973. The safety regulations demanded some changes to the FX4, including burst-proof door locks, a crash link in the steering and a steering wheel with a padded centre.

But the trade wanted more progress than this, including a new model of cab that did not squeak and rattle or let in rainwater. They said they could buy a Ford Zodiac for the same money and drive in comfort, but there was no money available for a new cab. Austin was now part of British Leyland and was losing money heavily. Carbodies had been acquired by Manganese Bronze Holdings PLC (MBH), which owned Norton motorcycles and had bought BSA for its motorcycle-making interests. But when MBH tried to rationalise its production by closing the Triumph factory at Meriden, Warwickshire, the unions organised a sit-in, followed by a takeover. This created havoc with production and deprived MBH of income that might have been reinvested in their other companies, including Carbodies.

Inflation pushed the price of an FX4 from £1,200 in 1971 to over £7,000 in 1980 and also eroded the value of a cab driver's takings. To add insult to injury, the government refused to allow sufficient fare increases. A practical difficulty was that taximeters were of an electro-mechanical type and every one had to be completely rebuilt, so as to register the new fare. It took nearly a year for all of the ten thousand plus cabs to be fitted with a new meter, and so in the meantime the new tariff was shown on a chart stuck to the partition, to which both passenger and driver could refer. These so-called 'bingo charts' caused endless arguments, but what made matters much worse at the time was that, rather than alter the meters three times during the 1970s, the meters remained at the 1974 increase but the bingo charts showed a tariff that was almost double. This problem was obviated by the introduction of electronic meters around 1980, when the tariff could be changed in seconds.

Opposite:
A 1978 Austin FX4 leaves Victoria station. Because of the increase in cab drivers throughout the 1970s and 1980s, and the commercial failure of the Carbodies FX4R, cabs of this age would remain in service until the 1990s.

Though outwardly very similar to the 1968 model, the Austin FX4 had, from late 1971, a larger, 2.5 litre diesel engine. The stainless steel sill cappings date from 1971.

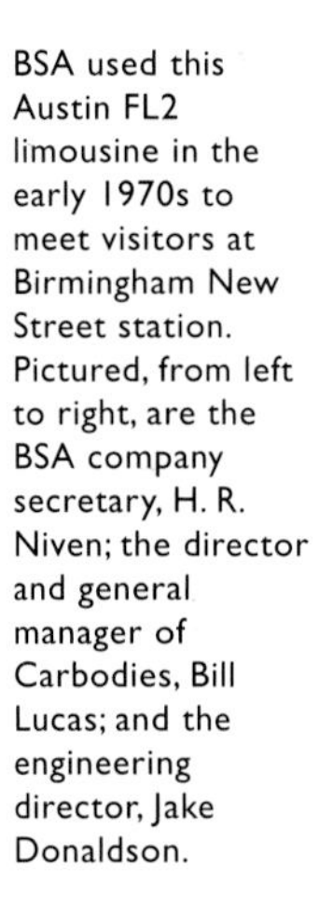
BSA used this Austin FL2 limousine in the early 1970s to meet visitors at Birmingham New Street station. Pictured, from left to right, are the BSA company secretary, H. R. Niven; the director and general manager of Carbodies, Bill Lucas; and the engineering director, Jake Donaldson.

Eventually, Carbodies decided to develop a completely new cab, which it called the FX5, on its own. However, the man behind it, Carbodies' managing director Bill Lucas, was forced to retire in 1979 through ill health, and his successor, Grant Lockhart, scrapped the FX5 in favour of a cab based on a Range Rover body. He called it the CR6. The FX4 was now the only vehicle made by Carbodies and to add value to it, as well as take advantage of changes to finance laws that permitted lease purchase and low-deposit credit sales, Lockhart and Mann & Overton gained approval from the Public Carriage Office for cabs to be fitted with vinyl roofs and sunshine roofs. Lockhart also introduced new colours, including midnight blue and light tan. There had been an increase in the number of cab drivers during the 1970s, because of increasing unemployment. Now that drivers were able to buy these new cabs and write the cost of the extras into the price, London saw a wide variety of colours besides black.

Top:
To commemorate the Silver Jubilee of Queen Elizabeth II in 1977, a number of FX4s were painted silver, with a royal crest applied to the front doors. The Prince of Wales invited cab-trade dignitaries to a function at Buckingham Palace, where he had the opportunity to drive one

Middle: The FX5 was Carbodies' attempt to produce a cab independent of Mann & Overton, which it felt was restricting vehicle development through insufficient funding and co-operation. A full-sized mock-up was made following the construction of this model, but the project was scrapped.

Bottom: A London taxi is often the first experience of Britain that visitors have, and from the mid 1980s there were different types of cab, and in colours other than black. Here, at the London City Airport, a royal burgundy FX4S-Plus (foreground) ranks up with a damson 1987 Reliant Metrocab.

But Lockhart had more difficult matters to deal with. Austin's parent company, British Leyland, had been in an almighty mess for most of the 1970s. It had been nationalised and the government appointed the industrialist Michael Edwardes to sort the company out, ready for privatisation. Another piece of European legislation, the European Whole Vehicle Type Approval, was imminent. British Leyland was now supplying only the FX4's mechanical components, and were not keen to spend money on qualifying the cab for the new rules. Lockhart bought the intellectual rights to the FX4, got it approved in Carbodies' own name and saved it from extinction. From May 1982 it became the Carbodies FX4, identical in every way to the Austin except for the badges. It would not be like that for long. Edwardes sold off the Austin diesel engine to India, leaving Lockhart with only one alternative: the Land Rover diesel. It seemed to work well in tests and, after a desperately short design time of just three months, the new model, the FX4R, went on sale in November 1982. In work, problems not found in the cab's short development time soon came to light. The engine was underpowered, became smoky and proved to be far too fragile, and Carbodies lost many potential sales. However, the FX4R had some good points, including power steering and full servo brakes – not discs, alas, but the light pedal pressure took a lot of the hard work out of driving what was a very heavy vehicle. There was an interesting result to these changes. Until then, there were few women cab drivers in London, as the FX4 was so hard to drive. The FX4R was much easier to handle, and more women signed on for the Knowledge and stayed in the trade.

The FX4R was introduced in late 1982. This version, pictured at Paddington station, is the HLS, with sunshine roof and vinyl roof, plus twin fog lights. It was distinguished from the Austin by different badges and two small blisters on the front of the bonnet to clear the power steering box.

1980 was the Year of the Disabled. The Department of Transport questioned a wide selection of disabled people about their transport needs, and most advocated giving priority to taxis: 'Even if the buildings are accessible to wheelchairs, the buses aren't and the pavements are so terrible we can't get out in the first place.' The Department of Transport's next move was to ask Carbodies if the FX4 could accept a wheelchair. Carbodies told the DoT that it could, but they were developing a new model, the CR6. A wheelchair fitted easily in one of the two prototypes, so both were put into wheelchair trials outside London. When they were returned to Carbodies, the modifications to the cab that were recommended would add a further year on the cab's introduction date, already delayed a year by the wheelchair trials. But, losing money on the FX4R and with the CR6 well behind schedule, Carbodies was in dire straits. Grant

Lockhart was replaced by Barry Widdowson, who made major changes to both the company and the cab. First he installed the latest Land Rover engine, which was far better, although by no means perfect. At the same time, MBH had bought Mann & Overton and formed London Taxis International (LTI). The new model, the FX4S, was the first cab to carry an LTI badge. Announcing the FX4S in November 1985, Mann & Overton said that 'with the FX4S, they have a vehicle that would see them well into the next century'. The remark, which implied the end of the CR6, was greeted with utter dismay by the trade. MBH actually announced the cancellation of the CR6 in January 1986, concluding its press release with the words: 'we are... finding that the export market is keen to retain the traditional lines of our vehicle and this has also influenced our final decision.'

Looming fast was the Metrocab, the first real rival to the Austin cabs for almost fifteen years. In the early 1980s, Metropolitan-Cammell-Weymann (MCW) recruited Geoff Chater from Carbodies and Bob Parsons from Peugeot-Talbot. Chater and Parsons designed the cab from the ground up, using a new chassis, a fibreglass body of modern design and a Ford Transit diesel engine. It was introduced in May 1987 and received a warm welcome. But would it be any good? In principle it was. It was draught- and leak-free; it was roomy, with a huge windscreen; it seated five passengers and its body could not rust. It was also fully wheelchair accessible, a requirement that would be mandatory by the beginning of 1989. The idea behind this was that people in wheelchairs should not have to pre-book every journey down to the last detail. They should be able to hail a cab on the street just like an able-bodied person.

The Metrocab's Achilles heel was its gearbox. A last-minute loss of their suppliers left Metrocab with no option but to put the cab into production

A scale model of the CR6, as announced to the trade in 1982. Its Range Rover origins are clear to see, although the grille and headlights were restyled to distinguish the two vehicles. The number plate represents what the letters 'CR' stand for: 'City Rover'.

Left: In introducing the Metrocab, Metropolitan-Cammell-Weymann planned to dominate the London market for both buses and cabs.

Below: This brochure picture for the Fairway was taken, appropriately, at the Royal and Ancient Golf Club at St Andrews, Scotland.

with a Ford automatic gearbox, which Ford itself had never fitted to a diesel engine in a road vehicle. It nearly broke Metrocab, for while it struggled to resolve the problems several MCW executives were dismissed and the company went into liquidation. The Metrocab business was sold to Reliant, which had actually been making the bodies.

The Metrocab's styling was modern, at a time when the newly formed LTI decided that traditional styling was the right way to go.

A 1989 LTI Fairway ranks behind a Carbodies FX4R. Note the Fairway's licence plate. The 'E' signifies that the cab is licensed to carry five passengers.

Metrocab's trouble was LTI's opportunity. The FX4S received a new, five-seat grey vinyl interior, resulting in a new model, the FX4S-Plus. Introduced in late 1987, it received a warm welcome, despite its being merely an improvement rather than a new design.

The next model from LTI, the Fairway, was introduced in February 1989. It was powered by a Nissan 2.7 litre diesel and came with the choice of a four-speed automatic or a five-speed manual gearbox. It was fast, quiet and smooth, and the trade loved it from the outset. It, too, had wheelchair accessibility, as required by law, and, although this was not quite as good as the Metrocab's, it was much appreciated by wheelchair users. The internal grab handles were of moulded red plastic, to be more visible to vision-impaired passengers.

Many of the top model, the 'Gold', with wooden door cappings and headrests in the rear, were sold as cab drivers began to enjoy a little comfort in their job. It replaced many of the old 1970s cabs, vehicles that had been kept going because the trade hated the FX4R and needed them for the ever increasing number of drivers passing through the Knowledge.

The Public Carriage Office began to allow the placing of advertisements on the front doors of cabs in 1982, later allowing them on both doors. All-over advertisements, called 'liveries', were permitted in 1990. Soon London's cabs could be seen in a variety of highly imaginative colours, such as this Guinness livery.

TXII

THE 1990s AND BEYOND

RELIANT did not hold on to Metrocab for long. The controlling company, which was based in property, suffered severe losses and in January 1991 Metrocab was sold to Hooper, which began a steady programme of improvements to the cab. These included disc brakes, the first to be fitted as standard equipment on a London cab, and the option of a six-seat model.

An improved Fairway, the Fairway Driver, introduced in 1992, featured all-new front suspension and front disc brakes. It also had a split rear seat, which enabled a wheelchair to be turned around more easily. A swivel seat and additional low step were also fitted to improve access for the less mobile. With the Fairway Driver London Taxis International began tapping into the provincial market they desperately needed, by persuading licensing authorities that they should license only cabs with wheelchair accessibility in their areas. Despite some fierce opposition from the provincial cab trade, LTI succeeded in making a substantial increase in their British market.

1994 saw the introduction of the complete newcomer, the Asquith. Designed to resemble a pre-war Austin, it had disc brakes all round, a Ford Transit diesel engine and Vauxhall axles. It was aimed at a niche market of drivers who used their cabs for weddings and guided tours but, at a basic price of £29,950, it cost at least £8,000 more than the Fairway Driver. Moreover, Asquith failed to recruit a dealer or service agent, leaving the few owners who bought them struggling to have their cabs serviced. Because of its high price and poor serviceability, only ten Asquith cabs were sold, a great disappointment to the company, which had hoped to sell many times that number. A mock-up of a modern-style cab was exhibited at the 1996 London Motor Fair. It would be made, Asquith said, in Sri Lanka and sell for £1,000 less than a Fairway or Metrocab, but nothing more was heard and the company went into voluntary liquidation in December 1998.

In 1995 Hooper introduced the Series II Metrocab, with a facelifted body and new interior. The Series III of 1997 had sixty-one detail improvements, including electric windows in the passenger doors. Metrocab was gaining ground on LTI, with 25 per cent of the London market.

Opposite:
LTI introduced the TX series in 1997. Its retro styling was deliberate, to ensure that the public would recognise it immediately, so familiar had the FX4's shape become. This model is a TXII, built between 2002 and 2007.

LTI introduced the Fairway Driver in February 1992. With new suspension and brakes it was as much an improvement as the original Fairway had been on the previous model. The 'Driver' is distinguished by its domed wheel trims and extruded mesh grille. This example is painted in a clever livery designed for American Airlines, blending the traditional black of London's cabs with the yellow of New York City.

At last, in November 1997 a replacement for the FX4 was announced. It was the TX1, and it had all the FX4's classic lines in a modern body, thus pleasing the export customers whom LTI had succeeded in securing, who insisted that the new cab retained the classic look that passengers loved and immediately recognised all around the world as a taxi. It inherited all the Fairway Driver's mechanical components in a slightly longer-wheelbase chassis. All doors were rearward-hinged. It seated five, plus a pull-down baby seat, and had electric windows all round. Here at last was a cab from LTI that did not rattle, squeak or let in rainwater. During the first full year, sales exceeded all previous records for a London cab. With it, export markets were consolidated, especially in Singapore and Germany.

New European Euro 3 exhaust emissions rules would outlaw both the Metrocab's Transit engine and the TX1's Nissan. Metrocab was first to respond, fitting a Toyota 2.4 litre turbo-diesel and matching transmissions. The new model, the TTT, was introduced in January 2001 and was regarded as the best ever Metrocab. But the company was heading for trouble, going into administration in 2003 as a result of having spent a large amount on developing a new cab that never came to fruition. The taxi-making business was sold off to KamKorp Europe Ltd, a division of a Singapore high-tech company.

LTI was lagging behind and had just a year to find a new engine. Only Ford was willing to co-operate with such a short development time, supplying a Ford Duratorq turbo-diesel for the new model, the TXII. It was introduced in February 2002, but, because of the short development period, problems with the timing chain and the driveline went unresolved for some time.

Crispin Reed, Asquith's marketing director, poses for the camera in the Asquith retro-style taxi. A landaulette version was also offered but could not be licensed in London like the fixed-head taxi.

Around 2002, a group of people involved in the provincial cab trade financed the conversion of Peugeot and Fiat light vans into wheelchair-accessible taxis. These were cheaper to buy and proved cheaper to run than either the TX1 or the Metrocab and sold well in the provincial market where the licensing authorities demanded wheelchair-accessible cabs. Now the producers turned their attentions to the London market, but the stumbling block was the 25-foot turning circle, which the conversion vehicles did not have. Taxi operators in the provinces do not share London's traditions or

The Metrocab Series 2 of 1995 featured much-restyled bodywork and a new interior.

A TXII in New York City. There had been several unsuccessful attempts to sell London cabs in the United States. This first attempt to sell the TX series would fail too, but LTI had much more ambitious plans for the future.

geographical constraints: for them, running taxis is about costs, and many undertake long-distance work. A Manchester cab may do two or three times as many miles in its lifetime as its London counterpart. The van shape of the alternatives is of no consequence to provincial operators when the vehicle costs less to buy, drives better through the open roads so quickly reached from Britain's smaller towns, and, with sky-high fuel prices, the fuel consumption is 30 per cent better.

After achieving sales success in the provinces, the producers of these so-called 'alternative' vehicles then turned their attention to London, but the stumbling block was the turning circle. They forced a review of the

The TX11 was based on the TX1 body and chassis. It differed little externally from the TX1, the most prominent difference being the one-piece glass in the passenger doors. As London's cabs had had internal electric door locks for the previous 20 years, these windows had restricted opening to prevent anyone climbing out to avoid paying the fare!

Conditions of Fitness, attempting to have this rule relaxed. A one-day test was conducted with a Peugeot E7, but it was found to be difficult to manoeuvre in such places as the entrance to the Savoy Hotel and Euston Station. In June 2003, Transport for London, who had taken control of the PCO in 2001 following the formation of the Greater London Authority, announced that the Conditions of Fitness would remain largely as they were, with the addition of two rules. One would demand a one-piece rear window, and the other, that if sliding doors were fitted, they should be power-assisted. The E7 had a two-piece rear door and sliding side doors with no power assistance. A legal challenge was mounted, and in mid-2005 these rules were removed, but the turning circle remained.

The traditional look perpetuated by the TX-series being hailed as an icon of London, it came as a surprise to the cab trade to hear at the end of June 2008 that a new cab, based on the Mercedes-Benz Vito Traveliner minibus had been type-approved for London by the PCO. To fulfil the turning circle

Metrocab's TTT was externally similar to the Series III, but powered by a Toyota turbo-diesel engine.

Left: The TX4 is LTI's latest model, introduced in February 2007. It has a new engine, from VM Motori of Italy, and new coil-spring rear suspension. The deeper grille is a nod to the old FX4's style.

Above: The current design of licence plate is computer-generated and includes the vehicle's index mark and the date of the expiry of the licence. Whereas the previous types of plate were used over again, these are used once and then destroyed.

requirement, the Vito has rear wheel steering, engineered by the specialist firm One80 in Coventry. It is powered by a 2.2-litre turbocharged diesel engine, and has a five-speed Tiptronic transmission. A full six-seater, it features all the mandatory equipment for disabled passengers, plus more luggage space in the boot than the TX-Series. It is more expensive than the TX4, but the dealers, KPM-UK plc, are confident that there will be a substantial numbers willing to pay a premium for Mercedes-Benz quality. How the public will react to such a different vehicle, especially as the Vito is used by a number of London private hire companies, is too early to say. As we said in our introduction, a ride in a London cab is like having a private limousine for just five or ten minutes. To many people, to change it would be almost like putting the guardsmen outside Buckingham Palace into camouflage kit: they're the same underneath, but they don't look the part.

LTI opened a factory in Shanghai, China, in 2008 in co-operation with Geely Automotive to make cabs for the Chinese and American markets. Pictured at the 2007 Shanghai Motor Show are Li Shufu, Geely's chairman (left), and John Russell, chief executive officer of Manganese Bronze, LTI's parent company.

The Mercedes-Benz Vito was type approved as a London taxi in June 2008. Based on the Vito Traveliner minibus, its styling is something of a departure from tradition.

Van-based vehicles notwithstanding, the short-term future for London taxis will be that they will stay the same as they have done, with diesel power and a limousine configuration, although in April 2008, LTI announced the electric TX4E, but with its 100-mile range believed it would only be of interest to 'a small group of drivers'. LPG engines have been tried by LTI but appear not to have any financial or environmental advantage. Nor is there any guarantee that a future government will not hike up the duty of LPG as was done in the early 1970s. Hybrid power is under review, and LTI is dealing with Azure Dynamics of Canada and Metrocab, despite not having marketed a cab for five years, and is also investigating a hybrid system.

And what of the long-term? The London taxi has, within its constraints, changed with the times without altering its basic concept and its accessibility, manoeuvrability and instant recognisability, but these benefits and the now-accepted traditional look of the London cab would be much missed by Londoners and visitors alike if they were abandoned completely.

FURTHER READING

Bobbit, Malcolm. *Taxi! The Story of the London Taxicab.* Veloce, 2002.

Buckland, Robert. *Share My Taxi.* Michael Joseph, 1968.

Clyde, Jack. *Glasgow Taxi.* Shepheard-Walwyn (Publishers) Ltd, 2004.

Eales, William. *London Taxis at War.* Eales, 2005.

Garner, Simon, and Stokoe, Giles. *Taxi!* Frances Lincoln, 2000.

Georgano, G. N. *A History of the London Taxicab.* David & Charles, 1972.

Gilbey, Sir Walter. *Early Carriages and Roads.* Vinton, 1903.

Marriott, Michael. *Desert Taxi.* Longmans, Green & Co, 1956.

Levinson, Maurice. *Taxi.* Secker & Warburg, 1963.

Levinson, Maurice. *The Taxi Game.* Peter Davies, 1973.

May, Trevor. *Gondolas and Growlers: The History of the London Horse Cab.* Alan Sutton, 1995.

May, Trevor. *Victorian and Edwardian Horse Cabs.* Shire, 1999.

Merkel, Ben, and Monier, Chris. *The American Taxi: A Century of Service.* Iconografix, 2006.

Moore, H. C. *Omnibuses and Cabs.* Chapman & Hall, 1902.

Munro, Bill. *Carbodies, the Complete Story.* Crowood, 1998.

Munro, Bill. *A Century of London Taxis.* Crowood, 2005.

Mustapha, Mus. *In a Year of a London Cabbie.* Orion, 2003.

Ward, Rod. *Taxi – Purpose-built Cabs in Britain.* Malvern House Publications, 2008.

Warren, Philip. *The History of the London Cab Trade.* Taxi Trade Promotions, 1995.

Warren, Philip, and Linskey, Malcolm. *Taxicabs – A Photographic History.* Almark, 1976.

Cabbies have always been a target of the press, of whatever persuasion, though not all tirades have been as delightful as this one!

PLACES TO VISIT

Few London taxicabs are to be seen in museums, although quite a number survive in private ownership. Among museums that have one or more taxis are:

Coventry Transport Museum, Millennium Place, Hales Street, Coventry CV1 1PN.
Telephone: 024 7623 4270. Website: www.transport-museum.com Email: enquiries@transport-museum.co.uk (Austin FX4.)

Glasgow Museum of Transport, 1 Bunhouse Road, Glasgow G3 8DP.
Telephone: 0141 287 2720. Website: www.glasgowmuseums.com (Beardmore Mk3 Hyper and a 1987 MCW Metrocab Series 1.)

London Transport Museum, 39 Wellington Street, London, WC2E 7BB.
Telephone: 020 73796344. Website: www.ltmuseum.co.uk (Austin 12/4 Low Loader and LTI TX4)

Museum of London, 150 London Wall, London EC2Y 5HN. Telephone: 020 7600 3699.
Website: www.museumoflondon.org (Horse-drawn hansom cab and a Unic 12/16.)

Myreton Motor Museum, Aberlady, East Lothian, Scotland EH32 0PZ.
Telephone: 01875 870288. (Beardmore Mark VII.)

National Motor Museum, John Montagu Building, Beaulieu, Brockenhurst, Hampshire SO42 7ZN. Telephone: 01590 612345.
Website: www.beaulieu.co.uk (1897 Bersey Electric, 1908 Unic 12/16 hp, 1997 LTI Fairway Driver.)

Privately owned London taxicabs can often be seen at vintage vehicle rallies throughout Great Britain, especially in the annual London to Brighton Run of the Historic Commercial Vehicle Society, which takes place on the first Sunday in May. The organisation for owners of these vehicles is the London Vintage Taxi Association, 51 Ferndale Crescent, Cowley, Uxbridge, Middlesex UB8 2AY. Website: www.lvta.co.uk.

INDEX

Page numbers in italic refer to illustrations